Bazaars to Brands

India's economy is a dynamic force on the global stage, characterised by a blend of traditional strengths and modern challenges. With a rich tapestry of history spanning millennia, India's economic landscape has evolved significantly, shaped by factors ranging from colonial rule to liberalization and globalization in recent decades. At its core, India boasts a diverse economic structure encompassing agriculture, manufacturing, and services. Agriculture, despite its decreasing contribution to GDP, remains crucial for employment, employing a significant portion of the population. The Green Revolution of the 1960s ushered in agricultural modernization, yet challenges such as small landholdings, inadequate infrastructure, and climate change persist. India's manufacturing sector, propelled by initiatives like 'Make in India,' seeks to transform the country into a global manufacturing hub. While strides have been made in industries like automobiles, pharmaceuticals, and electronics, achieving sustainable growth hinges on overcoming infrastructural bottlenecks, skill development, and regulatory reforms. The services sector, including IT, telecommunications, finance, and healthcare, has emerged as a cornerstone of India's economy, contributing substantially to GDP and employment. The IT industry, particularly software services and business process outsourcing (BPO), has garnered international acclaim, with cities like Bangalore and Hyderabad becoming global tech hubs. India's economic trajectory has been influenced by policy shifts, notably the liberalization reforms of 1991 that opened the economy to foreign investment and deregulation. This move spurred economic growth, attracting foreign capital, fostering technological advancement, and integrating India into the global economy. However, challenges such as income inequality, bureaucratic red tape, and infrastructure gaps remain impediments to inclusive growth. The demographic dividend, with a large youthful population, presents both opportunities and challenges. Leveraging this demographic advantage requires investments in education, healthcare, and skill development to harness the potential of India's workforce fully. Urbanization, driven by rural-urban migration, necessitates sustainable urban planning and infrastructure development to support growing urban populations. India's economic landscape is also shaped by its energy dynamics, with efforts towards renewable energy expansion alongside reliance on fossil fuels. Initiatives like the International Solar Alliance underscore India's commitment to sustainable development and climate action, aiming to balance economic growth with environmental stewardship. The global pandemic underscored vulnerabilities in India's economy, highlighting disparities in healthcare infrastructure, labour market resilience, and digital connectivity. Efforts towards economic recovery and resilience building include healthcare reforms, digital transformation initiatives, and enhancing social safety nets. Geopolitical dynamics further influence India's economic outlook, with strategic partnerships and regional integration initiatives playing pivotal roles. Initiatives such as the Belt and Road Initiative and the Indo-Pacific strategy shape India's trade and investment landscape, impacting economic diplomacy and regional stability. Challenges persist, including addressing rural distress, enhancing agricultural productivity, fostering innovation and entrepreneurship, and bridging regional disparities. Infrastructure development remains a priority, encompassing transportation, logistics, and digital connectivity to support economic growth and inclusivity. In conclusion, India's economic journey reflects a complex interplay of historical legacies, policy interventions, and global influences.

While strides have been made in various sectors, the path forward necessitates navigating challenges, harnessing demographic advantages, embracing technological innovation, and fostering sustainable development. With a resilient entrepreneurial spirit and strategic foresight, India continues to chart its course as a dynamic economic powerhouse on the global stage.

Bazaars to Brands_offers a captivating journey through India's diverse economic evolution landscape. This coffee table book celebrates the remarkable transformation of small, local enterprises into major global players. With rich visuals and insightful narratives, it chronicles the stories of brands that began as humble ventures and grew into influential icons on the world stage. Each section delves into the entrepreneurial spirit, innovative strategies, and cultural impact of these brands, reflecting the dynamic and rapidly evolving nature of India's economy. This collection is both a tribute to entrepreneurial success and a testament to the vibrant economic tapestry of India.

Disclaimer

This coffee table book is a creative project designed for informational and educational purposes. The content reflects the author's independent research, interpretation, and artistic perspective on the subject matter. It may not fully represent professional opinions, current industry standards, or real-life scenarios. All information and imagery are based on publicly available sources, historical references, or creative inspiration unless otherwise cited.

The views, interpretations, and conclusions expressed in this book are those of the author(s) and do not necessarily represent the opinions of any institution, organization, or external body. Any resemblance to actual persons, events, or entities is purely coincidental unless explicitly stated.

This coffee table book is not intended as a substitute for professional advice or consultation. Neither the author(s) nor the publisher assume any responsibility for actions or decisions made based on the content provided.

Acknowledgement

The creation of this coffee table book, *"Bazaars to Brands: India's Growth Story Through Individual Sellers, Medium, and Large Shops,"* has been an inspiring and fulfilling journey. This project would not have been possible without the encouragement, support, and contributions of many individuals.

First and foremost, I extend my deepest gratitude to **Yashi Shukla ma'am** for her invaluable guidance and insightful suggestions throughout the process. Her expertise and constructive feedback have greatly shaped the narrative and visual appeal of this book.

A heartfelt thank you goes to the individual sellers, shop owners, and entrepreneurs whose lives and businesses form the heart of this book. Their resilience, innovation, and spirit exemplify the transformation of India's retail landscape.

I am also grateful to my parents for their unwavering support, encouragement, and belief in my vision. Their guidance and constant motivation have been a cornerstone of my efforts and have inspired me every step of the way.

Finally, I want to acknowledge my role as the sole photographer for this book. Capturing the essence of India's bazaars and brands through my lens has been an incredible journey that I am proud to share with you all.

"Bazaars to Brands" is a labor of love and collaboration, and I am deeply thankful to everyone who has played a part in bringing this vision to life.

Divyam

SMALL BUSINESSES

India's small businesses are the lifeblood of its vibrant streets, weaving countless stories of resilience, creativity, and determination. Each bustling market, roadside stall, and hand-pulled cart represents more than just a place of trade—it is a testament to the entrepreneurial spirit that defines the nation. From the ice cream vendor who brings joy to children on sun-soaked afternoons to the toy seller crafting dreams for tiny hands, these enterprises add color, character, and a sense of humanity to everyday life.

These small ventures are often family-run, passed down through generations, and serve as both a livelihood and a legacy. They embody a unique blend of tradition and innovation, finding ways to adapt to changing times while preserving cultural roots. The chai seller offering steaming cups of tea on a crowded platform, the flower vendor decorating festivals and celebrations with vibrant blooms, and the street-side cobbler repairing shoes with skillful hands—each contributes to a shared tapestry of community and commerce.

Beyond their economic contributions, these businesses hold the power to inspire. They thrive against the odds, overcoming challenges such as limited resources, competition from larger players, and evolving consumer preferences. Yet, their perseverance and ingenuity enable them to carve out a space in India's bustling marketplaces, reminding us of the strength found in even the humblest ventures.

Together, these small businesses form an unbroken thread that connects people, places, and traditions. They foster relationships within communities, build trust through personal interactions, and keep alive the spirit of self-reliance and enterprise. In doing so, they are not just participants in India's economic story—they are its heart, exemplifying that even the smallest endeavors can leave a lasting impact.

BIGC
BIGC
SALE
50
SALE

SALE
DOORS
ONLY

PAAN
FIRE PAN
CHOCOLATE PAN
STRAWBERRY PAN
FLAVOUR PAN
PAAN

MEETHA
PAAN
REFRESHI
NDMC
APPROVED
TEHBAZARI
तम्बाकू जानलेवा है।

TRADERS
airtel 4G
YMADE GA
& ARMY STO
Air Cooler
paytm
Accepted Here
PhonePe

LILLOOR
32, Beador
High Cl
Synth
Stockist
DIMAPUR NAGALAND L
TATA
AGRICO
Available here

DIMAPUR CYCLE SHOP
cyclux
DIMAPUR CYCLE SHOP
HERO
HERO
CYCLES
World 1
DIEGO
POI NT
STORE

MEDIUM BUSINESSES

India's Medium Businesses showcase the dynamic heart of India's economy through its thriving medium-sized enterprises. This coffee table book offers a vivid exploration of how these businesses bridge the gap between small startups and large corporations, driving innovation and economic growth. Through stunning visuals and compelling stories, it highlights the journeys of medium-sized companies that havemade sig nificant impacts on their industries and communities. Discover how these enterprises balance ambition with resilience,India's medium businesses embody the dynamic core of the nation's economy, serving as vital bridges between small startups and large corporations. These thriving enterprises reflect the ambitious spirit of Indian entrepreneurship, showcasing innovation, resilience, and adaptability. Medium-sized businesses not only contribute significantly to the economy but also serve as catalysts for change, driving growth and fostering development across diverse sectors.

This coffee table book delves deep into the vibrant world of these enterprises, offering a vivid exploration of their unique journeys. Through a combination of stunning visuals and compelling narratives, it brings to life the stories of medium-sized companies that have left an indelible mark on their industries and communities. From pioneering sustainable manufacturing practices to revolutionizing service delivery, these businesses exemplify the ingenuity and perseverance that characterize India's entrepreneurial landscape.

Medium-sized enterprises often find themselves at a pivotal juncture—large enough to influence markets and communities but small enough to remain agile and responsive to change. This book captures how they navigate this unique position, balancing ambition with resilience. Readers will discover how these businesses overcome challenges such as scaling operations, accessing capital, and competing in a globalized marketplace, all while maintaining a steadfast commitment to quality and innovation.

These enterprises are more than just economic contributors; they are change-makers shaping the future of India's economic landscape. They create jobs, foster skill development, and introduce groundbreaking ideas that ripple across industries. Their stories are testaments to the power of vision and determination, inspiring readers to reimagine what is possible in the realm of business.

As you turn the pages of this book, you will uncover how medium-sized businesses seize opportunities to expand their reach and impact. Whether it's a family-owned manufacturing unit transforming into an international exporter or a regional tech firm scaling to compete on a national level, these enterprises embody the spirit of progress that propels India forward. They are not just a segment of the economy; they are the beating heart of a nation striving for inclusive and sustainable growth.

navigating challenges and seizing opportunities to shape the future of India's economic landscape.

TRAVELS
AIR
GURU NANAK STORE
GURU NANAK
STORE
CHAWLA CONFECTIONE
Birthday Cake
Pastry

Mango Shake
Banana Shake
Chocolate Shake
Cold Coffee

SALE
150

ngs
EMPORIUM
DEVAA ELECTRICALS

SALE
100/-
Pooh

LARGE BUSINESSES

The section on Large Businesses delves into the monumental powerhouses that drive India's economy forward, showcasing the remarkable stories of the country's largest and most influential companies. These corporate giants represent the pinnacle of innovation, strategic vision, and perseverance, standing as symbols of India's growing prominence on the global economic stage. Through their extraordinary achievements and transformative impact, they have not only shaped industries but also redefined the very fabric of commerce, both locally and globally.

This coffee table book provides an immersive and in-depth look at these trailblazing enterprises, offering readers a glimpse into their evolution, from their humble beginnings to their emergence as industry leaders. Through a combination of striking imagery and insightful narratives, it captures the essence of their journeys—highlighting the bold decisions, innovative strategies, and enduring commitment to excellence that have propelled them to the forefront of their respective sectors.

From multinational conglomerates steering advancements in technology, pharmaceuticals, and energy, to legacy companies preserving cultural heritage while embracing modernity, this section celebrates the diversity and dynamism of India's largest businesses. These companies have not only contributed substantially to GDP and employment but have also left an indelible mark on global markets, fostering trade, investment, and innovation.

The book also sheds light on the broader impact of these corporations, exploring how they influence society and the environment through corporate social responsibility initiatives, sustainability efforts, and community engagement programs. Their stories reveal a commitment to inclusive growth, where economic success is intertwined with social progress and environmental stewardship.

By delving into the achievements of these corporate giants, readers will gain a deeper understanding of how large businesses have shaped India's economic growth, enhanced its global standing, and inspired future generations of entrepreneurs. This section is not just a celebration of corporate success; it is a tribute to the vision, resilience, and ingenuity that define India's journey towards becoming a global economic powerhouse.

Haldiram's
WELCOME TO THE
WORLD OF
AUTHENTIC TASTE

HERE

Chetak
CHETA
HAMA
KAL

Chetak
ALWAYS
CONNECTED
IP-67
RATED WATER
PROTECTION
EXT
SERV
NETW
ALL
META
FULLY LIFEPROOF

Chetak
ALWAYS
CONNECTED
EXTENSIVE
SERVICE
NETWORK
IP 67
ATED WATER
PROTECTION
ALL
METAL BOD
FULLY LIFEPROOF

THE
HEELS

Reebok
EXIT
Life Is Not A Spectator Sport.
Reebok
EXCITING
SUMMER
OFFERS
COMFORT
ENGINEERED
DMX COMFORT+
SPACEFOAM
DMX

U.S. POLO ASSN
SINCE 1890
JAINSON
Road Trip

गो कलर्स !
GO COLORS!
GO COLORS
GO COLORS!
Happy Mother's Day!
GO COLORS!
IT'S
SUMMER
TIME!
PUSH

Panchayat
INDIAN CHOCOLATE PAAN
Panchayat
91
Jooro
India's First Paan Parlour

elatoes
Stelatoes
Stelatoes
Men's
RANGE
STARTS
@ ₹499
Kids
Stelatoes
Men's Footwear
₹599
WINTER SALE
UP TO
50% OFF
BBR RETAIL

CULTURAL BUSINESSES

The Indian economy presents a complex picture, with unique ways for people in the Northeast to sustain their livelihoods. This includes practices deeply rooted in their culture and traditions. Importantly, these practices are not indicative of animal cruelty but rather represent their way of life and cultural heritage.

The majority of the population in this region resides in the "Seven Sister States" of Arunachal Pradesh, Assam, Manipur, Meghalaya, Mizoram, Nagaland, and Tripura, along with the "Brother" state of Sikkim. Many indigenous communities here follow tribal customs, which include consuming the meat of various animals as part of their traditional diet. These practices have been passed down through generations and continue to hold cultural significance to this day.

Conclusion:
A Celebration of Enterprise and Culture

From the bustling bazaars to the towering skyscrapers housing global corporations, India's economic journey is a testament to its resilience, creativity, and indomitable spirit. This coffee table book, *Bazaars to Brands*, has explored the heart of India's economic landscape, showcasing the evolution of small businesses, medium enterprises, and corporate giants, each playing a vital role in the nation's growth.

The stories within these pages highlight more than just economic milestones; they celebrate the people behind the progress—the entrepreneurs, workers, and dreamers who embody the essence of India's vibrant marketplace. From the artisanal stalls of local bazaars to the boardrooms of global powerhouses, their shared pursuit of innovation, determination, and excellence resonates as a universal human endeavor.

As we reflect on the Northeast's unique cultural practices and the enduring traditions across India, we are reminded of the harmonious interplay between heritage and progress. India's economic narrative is one of contrasts: tradition meets innovation, challenges spark solutions, and local dreams inspire global impact.

This book is a tribute to India's entrepreneurial spirit and cultural diversity. It invites readers to honor the past, embrace the present, and look forward to a future defined by sustainable development, inclusivity, and creativity. Together, these elements weave a story of hope and potential—a story that continues to inspire and shape India's place on the global stage.

www.ingramcontent.com/pod-product-compliance
Lightning Source LLC
Chambersburg PA
CBHW041602110726
48005CB00002B/263